Elon Musk

Man of Vision and Controversy

John Allen

ReferencePoint Press®

San Diego, CA

Printed in the United States

For more information, contact:
ReferencePoint Press, Inc.
PO Box 27779
San Diego, CA 92198
www.ReferencePointPress.com

LIBRARY OF CONGRESS CATALOGING-IN-PUBLICATION DATA

Names: Allen, John , author.
Title: Elon Musk : man of vision and controversy / by John Allen.
Description: San Diego, CA : ReferencePoint Press, 2024. | Includes bibliographical references and index.
Identifiers: LCCN 2023001004 (print) | LCCN 2023001005 (ebook) | ISBN 9781678205669 (library binding) | ISBN 9781678205676 (ebook)
Subjects: LCSH: Musk, Elon--Juvenile literature. | Businessmen--United States--Biography--Juvenile literature. | Engineers--United States--Biography--Juvenile literature. | Inventors--United States--Biography--Juvenile literature. | SpaceX (Firm)--Juvenile literature. | Tesla Motors--Juvenile literature.
Classification: LCC HC102.5.M88 A55 2023 (print) | LCC HC102.5.M88 (ebook) | DDC 338.7/66392092 [B]--dc23/eng/20230302
LC record available at https://lccn.loc.gov/2023001004
LC ebook record available at https://lccn.loc.gov/2023001005

Contents

A Tech Wizard Out to Save the World

In the fall of 2022, the billionaire tech engineer and chief executive officer (CEO) Elon Musk found himself, as usual, in the news. His controversial purchase of the social media site Twitter for $44 billion was being condemned as reckless and dangerous to national discourse. He faced an upcoming court case in Delaware over claims that the board of Musk's electric vehicle (EV) company, Tesla, was massively overpaying him. Meanwhile, Tesla was rolling out a new electric semitrailer truck, and his commercial spaceflight company, SpaceX, was in contract talks with the National Aeronautics and Space Administration (NASA) for a moon-landing project. Amid all the activity and turmoil, Musk admitted he might be overdoing things a bit. "My workload has recently increased quite a lot," he announced via satellite during a November 14 business conference in Indonesia. "I have too much work on my plate, that's for sure."[1]

A Tech Entrepreneur With a Mission

Musk's sometimes frenzied activity is a product of his intense curiosity about the world. Since boyhood he has developed an engineer's fascination with how things work—and how they could be made to work better. Musk grew up as a tech nerd in Pretoria, South Africa. He would take refuge from bullies by playing video games for hours alone in his bedroom. He became fascinated with computers and programming, and he even invented a video game of his own. He immersed himself in the digital revolution that would help him make his mark on the world.

At age seventeen, Musk decided to immigrate to North America. He eventually made it to California's Silicon Valley, where he became a tech entrepreneur with a mission to save the world. He believed that humanity needed an escape plan should an environmental catastrophe make the earth unlivable. That sparked his creation of the rocket company SpaceX and its goal of sending astronauts to Mars and beyond. As SpaceX grew to become the world's dominant private space company, Musk did not waver in his ambitions. "A lot of other space companies are trying to win contracts," says Jonathan McDowell, an astrophysicist at the Harvard-Smithsonian Center for Astrophysics. "SpaceX is trying to get to Mars. It turns out that having a goal can be economically successful."[2]

> **"A lot of other space companies are trying to win contracts. SpaceX is trying to get to Mars. It turns out that having a goal can be economically successful."[2]**
>
> —Jonathan McDowell, an astrophysicist at the Harvard-Smithsonian Center for Astrophysics

Musk also sought to fight climate change by building carbon-free EVs with his automotive firm, Tesla. He set himself the task of reinventing the car business much as he had the business of spaceflight. By 2022 he had presided over a period of explosive growth for Tesla. Its stock value soared to the hundreds of billions, making Musk one of the richest people in the world.

Along the way, Musk has amassed many dedicated followers, his so-called Musketeers. They delight in his visions of the future, unpredictable behavior, and verbal potshots at the establishment. They compare him to Tony Stark, the billionaire tech engineer who is also the superhero Iron Man in the Marvel movies. Typical among Musk fans is Keith Muelas, a twenty-seven-year-old video game developer. As Muelas says, "Even though the guy seems insane at times, there's a super-genius aspect behind him and his beliefs."[3]

SpaceX chief executive Elon Musk addresses the news media following a successful launch of his company's Falcon Heavy rocket. Under Musk's leadership, SpaceX has grown to become the world's dominant private space company.

A Fierce Drive to Succeed

Elon Musk's drive to succeed affects every aspect of his life, including his personal and professional relationships. Always in search of a better, more efficient way of doing things, he can be an extremely difficult boss. His impatience is legendary. He demands long hours and dedication from his workers, often at the expense of family life and outside interests. He is known for stocking his breakrooms with free soda machines—not to be generous but rather to keep his employees caffeinated and alert for late nights on the job.

Despite Musk's sometimes bruising management style, he can also inspire tremendous loyalty in his staff members. In the early years of SpaceX, he and one of his top engineers did not speak for over a year after Musk blamed the man for a parts failure that spoiled a crucial rocket launch. But when the next launch went off without a hitch, the two hugged each other and everything was forgotten.

A Magnet for Controversy

Through it all, Musk has learned to live with perpetual controversy. On October 28, 2022, when his buyout of Twitter became final, opponents unleashed a storm of protests and criticism. Musk's plan to reinstate certain users who previously had been banned brought accusations that the site would now be filled with hate speech and misinformation. Many longtime users fled to other sites. Advertisers also abandoned Twitter, threatening major losses in revenue, even as Musk fired the company's top executives and nearly half its employees. Some questioned whether Twitter could survive its new owner's impulsive policy changes.

> "[It's] his core competence. It's his magic. He may be thinking, 'I've always been good at this. Now if I own my own platform, where can I take things?'"[4]
>
> —Michael Dunne, financial analyst

But Musk seemed unfazed by all the turmoil. He believes he can mold public opinion despite his critics. "[It's] his core competence. It's his magic," says financial analyst Michael Dunne. "He may be thinking, 'I've always been good at this. Now if I own my own platform, where can I take things?'"[4] The answer to that question may excite Musk's true believers, but it leaves others uneasy about what might come next.

CHAPTER ONE

From South Africa to Silicon Valley

Elon Reeve Musk was born on June 28, 1971, in Pretoria, South Africa. His mother, the former Maye Haldeman, is a Canadian-born model and dietitian. His father, Errol, is a native South African engineer and property developer. Elon has a younger brother, Kimbal, and a younger sister, Tosca. Elon's unusual first name comes from his great-grandfather on his mother's side, John Elon Haldeman. Musk's grandfather and personal hero, Joshua Norman Haldeman, was an eccentric who worked as a farmer, construction laborer, and rodeo performer prior to becoming a chiropractor and pilot. Moving his family from Canada to South Africa on a whim was typical of the elder Haldeman's frontier spirit. Musk seems to have inherited the Haldemans' unquenchable thirst for risk-taking and adventure.

Musk's parents were raised in the same neighborhood in Pretoria and met as children. Years later, they carried on a seven-year courtship before Errol finally convinced Maye to marry him in 1970. Her reluctance may have been due to Errol's prickly personality. Family members agree that Elon's father is a difficult person with a knack for spreading misery. The marriage lasted nine years. During that time, Elon saw little of his busy parents and spent lots of time on his own. "I didn't really have a primary nanny or anything," he once told an interviewer. "I just had a housekeeper who was there to make sure I didn't break anything. She wasn't, like, watching me. I was off making explosives and reading books and building rockets and doing things that could have gotten me killed. I'm shocked that I have all my fingers."[5]

Raised on Books and Computer Games

Following their parents' divorce, Elon and his siblings initially moved with Maye to a family home in Durban. However, at age ten Elon decided that he felt sorry for his father and moved back to his house. The move undoubtedly helped shape his character and ambition. But it also produced some of the loneliest and unhappiest times of his life. His relationship with his father was filled with tension. "He's good at making life miserable—that's for sure. . . . He's not a happy man," Elon says of his father. "I don't know how someone becomes like he is. It would just cause too much trouble to tell you any more."[6] Years later, Musk and his first wife, Justine, would agree not to introduce Errol Musk to their children.

Pictured is seventeen-year-old Elon Musk in 1989 (right), with his sister, Tosca, and his brother, Kimbal. They grew up in Pretoria, South Africa.

Nonetheless, young Elon kept himself entertained. Musk has often said he was raised by books, not people. He particularly enjoyed science fiction, such as Isaac Asimov's Foundation series and Douglas Adams's *The Hitchhiker's Guide to the Galaxy*. The Asimov books describe a visionary who plots to save humanity by dispatching crews of scientists to colonize faraway planets—an idea that would inspire Elon's forays into space. Another favorite genre was tales of heroic quests such as JRR Tolkien's *The Lord of the Rings.* He also read through encyclopedias to satisfy his curiosity about the world and the universe. His photographic memory helped him soak up facts that never left him. He became a bit of a know-it-all among his family members and schoolmates. Once, when his little sister wondered how far it was from the earth to the moon, Elon answered with both the distance at perigee (when the moon is closest to Earth) and at apogee (when it is farthest away).

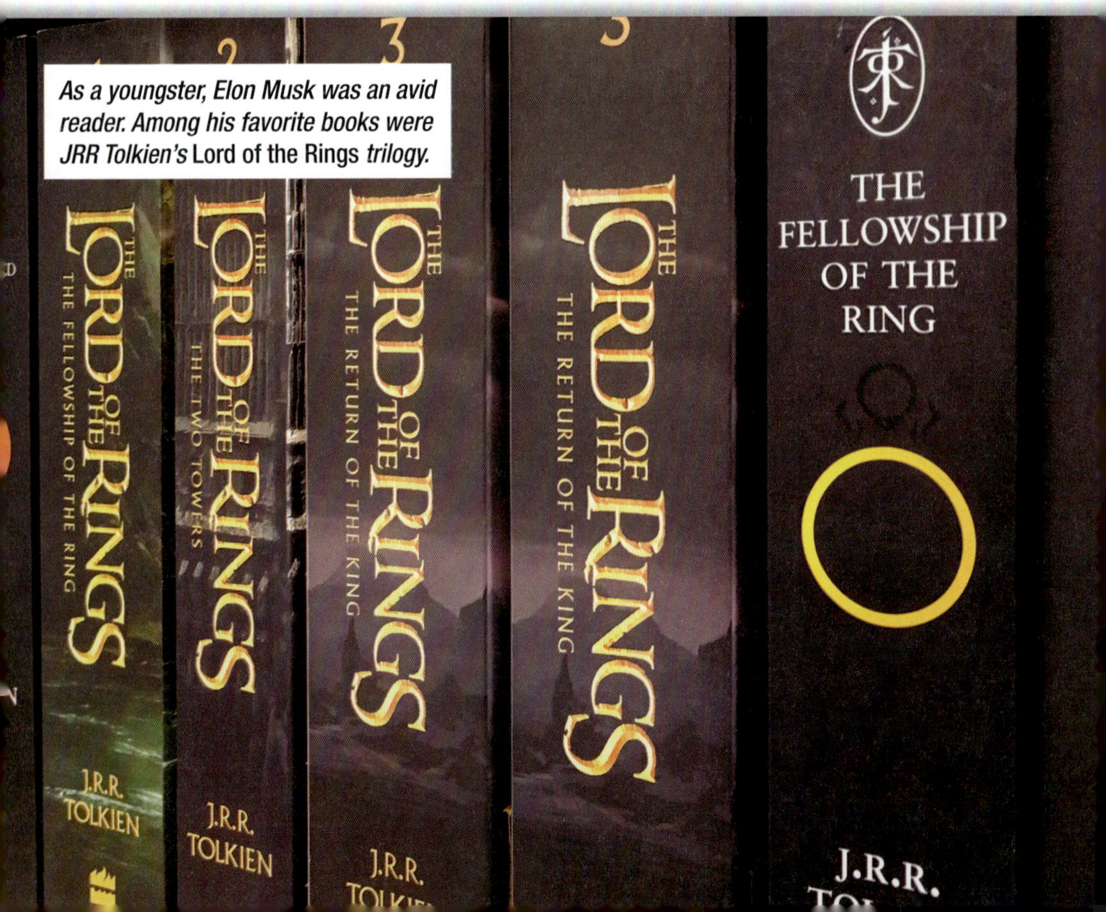

As a youngster, Elon Musk was an avid reader. Among his favorite books were JRR Tolkien's Lord of the Rings *trilogy.*

For all of Errol Musk's failings as a father, he did keep Elon supplied with the latest technological gadgets, including an early personal computer. Elon promptly became obsessed with the device, spending hours peering at its screen. Typically, he did not stop at simply playing computer games. He taught himself how to code and went on to create *Blastar*, a sci-fi space-shooter game. The twelve-year-old inventor then sold the game's code to a South African computer magazine for $500.

Lessons in Business and Troubles at School

Musk did not spend all his time cooped up in his bedroom. His father would occasionally take him along on trips overseas. When Kimbal joined Elon to live at Errol's house, the two brothers collaborated on schemes to make money. For example, they decorated Easter eggs and sold them to rich neighbors at ten to twenty times their cost. They also tried to set up their own video arcade, falling short only when they could not find someone over age twenty-one to sign the building lease. Another time, the brothers traveled by train with their cousins to Johannesburg for a tournament of the role-playing game *Dungeons & Dragons*. Elon used his knack for strategy and his wild imagination to earn first prize.

The brothers learned a great deal about how mechanical things worked from their father, who was a talented engineer. Errol would bring the boys along when he visited job sites. He would show them how to lay bricks, install windows, and put in electrical wiring and plumbing fixtures. When he asked questions, they were expected to figure out the answers. Elon later described these days as some of the most enjoyable he spent with his father.

School presented a whole different set of problems. Elon kept to himself, and no one thought he was especially bright. He was smaller and weaker than most of his classmates. Moreover, he had a longtime habit of going into a semitrance when he was working out a problem or thinking hard about something.

An Emerald Mine and the Self-Made Billionaire

Elon Musk grew up in South Africa at a time when apartheid still ruled. This was a government system of discrimination, segregation, and violence toward the nation's Black-majority population. Musk's father, Errol, claims to have opposed apartheid and to have won election as a Pretoria city councillor to work against the racist system. Yet rumors persist that the elder Musk made his fortune in part from shares in a South African emerald mine worked by Black laborers under apartheid. Some have ridiculed Elon's story that he is a self-made billionaire. Instead, they say he relied on his father's "apartheid emerald-mine" wealth to start his career.

According to research by Snopes, a fact-checking site, these critics are mostly mistaken. Errol Musk did apparently own some shares in an emerald mine. However, the mine was in Zambia, not South Africa, and had nothing to do with apartheid. Errol held the shares for only a short time during the 1980s. Moreover, Elon has repeatedly said that he began his business career with $100,000 of college debt and no family assistance. According to biographer Ashlee Vance, "For what it's worth, my reporting, based on conversations with hundreds of people, confirms Musk's story. Regardless of your opinion of him, he is a self-made billionaire."

Quoted in Jordan Liles, "What We Know About Elon Musk and the Emerald Mine Rumor," Snopes, November 17, 2022. www.snopes.com.

In this state, he did not respond even when someone practically shouted in his ear. When he had first started spacing out this way as a young child, his mother even had him checked for deafness.

Musk's eccentric behavior made him an easy target for bullies. One day a gang of kids came upon Elon and Kimbal while they were eating lunch at the top of a stairwell at school. One boy punched Elon, and another shoved him down the stairs. The gang then began kicking and punching him when he tumbled to the bottom. He was kicked in the face so hard that his nose was broken. Kimbal thought his bloody, swollen face looked like he had lost a boxing match. "For some reason, they decided that I was it, and they were going to go after me nonstop," recalls Musk. "That's what made growing up difficult. For a number of years, there was no respite. You get chased around by gangs at school who tried to beat the s— out of me, and then I'd come home, and it would be awful there as well. It was just like nonstop horrible."[7] The beatings did not stop until Elon had a growth spurt around age fifteen and he took martial arts classes to learn some rudiments of self-defense.

Immigrating to North America

When he was seventeen, Elon Musk made a life-changing decision to immigrate on his own to North America. In June 1989 he flew to Canada, where a new law enabled him to claim his mother's citizenship. For a year, he traveled around taking odd jobs, including shoveling out grain bins on a cousin's farm in Saskatchewan and chainsawing logs in Vancouver. Eventually he enrolled at Queen's University in Kingston, Ontario. There, he met Justine Wilson, a literary and artistic type with whom he shared a class in abnormal psychology. The two started dating off and on, but when her interest seemed to be waning, Musk refused to let her go. "He would call very insistently," she said later. "You always knew it was Elon because the phone would never stop ringing. The man does not take no for an answer."[8] Although it took nearly a decade, Justine would eventually become Musk's first wife.

Musk spent two years at Queens before he achieved his real objective, which was getting to the United States. He transferred to the University of Pennsylvania on scholarship. At the Ivy League school, he earned dual degrees in economics and physics. For the first time in his life, he felt comfortable and confident among other students, maybe because so many of the physics majors were a lot like him. He loved the challenging material, even when it kept him up at night studying. "Senior year quantum mechanics at Penn was the hardest class I ever took," Musk recalled years later. "That stuff will mess with your mind."[9]

> **"He would call very insistently. You always knew it was Elon because the phone would never stop ringing. The man does not take no for an answer."[8]**
>
> —Justine Wilson, Elon Musk's first wife

During summer break in 1994, Kimbal joined his brother for a cross-country road trip to see America. On the way, they discussed how they could take advantage of business opportunities in the wake of the internet's potential for growth. The trip was like a test run for Elon's next destination: Silicon Valley.

Jumping into the Dot-Com Boom

An ambitious, risk-taking, tech-minded person like Elon Musk could scarcely have chosen a better time to relocate to Northern California than 1995. The internet and the tools to navigate it were just coming into their own. Untapped possibilities seemed to be everywhere as tech entrepreneurs figured out ways to digitize—and monetize—the most basic activities of daily life, from shopping to travel to entertainment. Companies would be formed on only the basis of an idea and a bank of personal computers, only to be sold within a couple of years for millions. Investors competed to find the next big thing. Settling in Palo Alto, Musk considered getting an advanced physics degree at Stanford University. But first, he spent the summer months making connections in Silicon Valley, the center of the technology boom on the West Coast. With his usual burst of energy, he obtained internships at two start-up tech companies, one during the day and the other at night.

One day a Yellow Pages telephone directory salesman showed up to urge Musk's employer, an energy storage company, to buy a listing online as well as the usual print listing. Musk noticed at once that the salesman was struggling to explain what he was selling. Later, Elon told Kimbal that he had found the perfect idea for their own dot-com breakthrough.

The brothers set about planning an online directory for cities, like an internet version of the Yellow Pages but with added frills and features. They rented a small office space in Palo Alto, which doubled as an apartment for the cash-strapped pair. They lived on fast food and showered at the local YMCA. Elon dived into the task of creating software for the new website. He obtained rights to a trove of digital maps and GPS directions for free, and then

A Personal Tragedy

Amid the furor over the sale of PayPal to eBay, Elon Musk and his wife, Justine, suffered a loss that made the business news seem unimportant. One afternoon in May 2002, the couple had tucked in their ten-week-old son, Nevada, for a nap. When they checked on him a while later, he was not breathing. Paramedics were able to resuscitate the infant, but lack of oxygen had left him brain dead. He survived for three days on life support in an Orange County hospital before the Musks decided it was no use. Doctors found the cause of death to be sudden infant death syndrome.

Justine made no attempt to hide her grief, but Elon refused to talk about it. "Elon made it clear that he did not want to talk about Nevada's death," Justine wrote later in a magazine article. "I didn't understand this, just as he didn't understand why I grieved openly, which he regarded as 'emotionally manipulative.'" She attributed Elon's reaction to a defense mechanism dating back to his difficult childhood. The couple went on to have five more children before they divorced in 2008.

Quoted in Maroosha Muzaffar, "Elon Musk's Ex-Wife Refutes His Claim That Firstborn Child Died in His Arms," Yahoo! News, November 29, 2022. http://news.yahoo.com.

set about making the graphics look more impressive for home users. He added smaller cities and suburban areas to the database. Elon worked long hours with little rest, often curling up on a beanbag beside his desk for a little sleep before returning to the keyboard.

It took several years, a slate of investors, and some new software engineers to develop the idea and market it to potential customers. The final product was an online city guide aimed at newspapers. The directory linked to a map of various businesses, such as clothing stores, gas stations, restaurants, hairdressers, bowling alleys, and hardware stores. They named the company Zip2 because the user could *zip to* here and *zip to* there on the website. Users could not only look up a business but also receive detailed directions on how to get there. This latter innovation became a standard feature for map applications online. It was the sort of practical step that brought home how useful the internet could be, even for people who were not particularly tech savvy. Newspapers found Zip2 to be an essential web resource for their advertisers and subscribers.

In 1999, the Compaq Computer Corporation bought Zip2 for $307 million. Once the investors were paid off, Elon's share of the remaining profits was $22 million, with Kimbal earning $15 million. Elon had at last joined the ranks of the dot-com millionaires. He splurged on a new home and a McLaren F1, which was then the world's fastest car. But he was already planning his next business venture.

Putting Banking Services Online

In search of another industry that was swimming in cash and ripe for reinvention, Musk hit on banking and finance. His stint as an intern at the Bank of Nova Scotia during the early 1990s had convinced him that a company able to provide banking services online could disrupt the industry and earn its creators a fabulous return. To do so, however, they would have to overcome the public's wariness. People were just starting to get comfortable with ordering books and household items online via a credit card. They might balk at doing their banking or accessing their personal financial data on the internet.

Musk's disruptive idea was called X.com, which he launched in March 1999. He envisioned the company as an online bank providing checking and savings accounts, loans, brokerage services, and insurance. Sinking $12 million of his Zip2 profits into the enterprise, he became X.com's largest shareholder. He immediately began to search out software engineers and venture capitalists who could help make his concept a reality. Musk also relied on what he had learned about leading a team at Zip2, including both his strengths and weaknesses. Mostly, however, he improvised his strategy, acting on impulse and trusting his own judgment. "I don't really have a business plan," he said years later. "I had a business plan way back in the Zip2 days. But these things are always wrong, so I just didn't bother with business plans after that."[10]

"I don't really have a business plan. I had a business plan way back in the Zip2 days. But these things are always wrong, so I just didn't bother with business plans after that."[10]

—Elon Musk

Thrown Out in a Corporate Coup

Early in 2000, X.com merged with a competitor named Confinity, which had developed a successful person-to-person online payment system called PayPal. The merger seemed like a good idea at the time, but it quickly led to friction between the head of Confinity, Peter Thiel, and Musk. Thiel and Musk clashed over PayPal's future, and the cultures of the two businesses just did not mix. In September, when Musk left for a delayed honeymoon in Australia with his new wife, Justine, Thiel and the company's board staged a coup and ousted Musk as CEO.

To make matters worse, on a second honeymoon trip to South Africa in December, Musk caught a rare and deadly form of malaria, which was misdiagnosed when he and Justine returned to Palo Alto. Musk spent ten days in the intensive care unit before a visiting doctor recognized his illness and gave him the proper treatment that saved his life. "That's my lesson for taking a vacation," the workaholic Musk joked. "Vacations will kill you."[11]

Elon Musk (right) and entrepreneur Peter Thiel (left) briefly collaborated in 2000 to run the online payment system PayPal.

In 2002, Thiel and his partners sold PayPal for $1.5 billion to its chief client, the online auction site eBay. Musk disagreed with the move, but by that time he had little say in the matter. Even though he walked away with $175 million to salve his ego, it felt like a failure. Meanwhile, the dot-com bubble had burst. The values of many overpriced internet companies plummeted, and investors who were slow to react got stuck with millions in losses. Musk decided to abandon Silicon Valley for Los Angeles and focus on a childhood dream: building a rocket to Mars.

CHAPTER TWO

The Pursuit of Commercial Space Travel

In 2001 Elon Musk had Mars on the brain. Having escaped the high-pressure lifestyle of Silicon Valley, he was looking for a new venture, one with more significance for the world than another dot-com business. It would involve spaceflight to another planet, like the sci-fi stories he had devoured as a kid. Moving down the coast to Los Angeles, he sought like-minded people who believed that humankind's future lay in outer space. The city, with its mild, calm climate, had been an aeronautics center since the 1920s, when the Lockheed Aircraft Company had located near Hollywood. It featured a mix of serious space-industry heavyweights from NASA and Boeing and novices with big dreams such as Musk himself. When Musk learned of a $500-a-plate dinner hosted by the Mars Society, a group of engineers and wealthy space enthusiasts, he showed up uninvited and handed the host a check for $5,000. He learned about the group's research center in the Arctic, which was designed to mimic the harsh conditions astronauts would face on the Red Planet. Musk liked what he heard so much that he ponied up another $100,000 donation. Soon his ideas for a commercial rocket company began to take shape.

A Rocket Company with a Difference

Musk had long believed that humankind would need to expand beyond Earth to ensure its own survival. In his view, extinction-level threats such as nuclear war, a global pandemic, or a meteor strike like the one that wiped out the dinosaurs made space exploration and setting up colonies on other worlds not just an interesting project but an urgent necessity. Consulting NASA's website to see its plans for sending people to Mars, Musk was shocked to find nothing on the subject. He could not understand why America's space program seemed to have lost its adventurous spirit. "At first I thought, jeez, maybe I'm just looking in the wrong place," Musk told the tech magazine *Wired.* "Why was there no plan, no schedule? There was nothing. It seemed crazy."[12]

After moving to Los Angeles, Elon Musk sought out other people who were captivated as he was by the idea of sending people to Mars (shown).

A Tiny Nut and a Major Blowup

The failure of SpaceX's first attempt to launch its Falcon 1 rocket also demonstrates how challenging it can be to work for Elon Musk. Just hours after the Falcon 1 broke apart during liftoff, engineers found that the problem was a single aluminum nut in the rocket's fuel line assembly. The faulty nut caused a fuel leak that ended in a fiery crash.

If something goes wrong, it is Musk's habit to identify the person responsible and vent his frustration. In this case, he blamed Jeremy Hollman, one of his top technicians, for the oversight. Hollman had earlier drawn Musk's anger by missing a launch test due to his long-scheduled wedding. When Hollman saw news reports in which Musk singled him out for the failed launch, he blew up. He marched into Musk's office in El Segundo and demanded an apology. Things got so heated that Hollman had to be pulled away from Musk's desk.

Later investigations of the rocket found that the culprit was not Hollman but the salt spray on the island launch site. The ocean breeze had corroded the nut, leading to its failure. "That was just bad freaking luck," said chief engineer Tom Mueller. "The worst luck in the world."

Quoted in Eric Berger, *Liftoff: Elon Musk and the Desperate Early Days That Launched SpaceX*. New York: HarperCollins, 2021, p. 122.

Musk decided that it was up to a private company to take the lead and rally the public's interest in space exploration. Entering the space industry would be hugely expensive, but he had millions from the sale of PayPal to fund his project. At first, he considered buying and refurbishing Russian ballistic missiles, but that option was too expensive and the Russians too hard to work with. He consulted with engineers and scientists, including some from NASA's Jet Propulsion Laboratory, to learn more about the business of rockets. He pored over books such as *Fundamentals of Astrodynamics* to acquaint himself with the technical aspects of rocketry. Many space experts rolled their eyes at Musk's ideas about going to Mars, viewing him as one more egomaniac millionaire out to conquer space. Some of his friends worried that his bout with malaria had not only left him looking thin and weak but also had affected his mind.

However, Musk had not lost his hard-edged, practical side. He understood that even a business based on a dream had to make money. He also recognized that large rocket companies in

Europe were already making tidy sums launching satellites into space. If Musk could provide the same service on schedule at a much cheaper price, he could corner a large share of the commercial rocket business. Focusing on smaller payloads, like the communication satellites then being developed, would likely attract lots of new clients. He pitched his ideas to bright young aerospace engineers such as Tom Mueller and Chris Thompson, who were intrigued by the prospect of disrupting the space industry. They were also impressed when Musk showed them a spreadsheet he had compiled detailing the actual costs of building and launching a rocket. It was obvious that Musk was not just a rich dilettante—he was prepared to put in the long hours required to make such a risky venture succeed. The team set up shop in a run-down warehouse in the Los Angeles suburb of El Segundo. On May 6, 2002, Musk founded Space Exploration Technologies, or SpaceX.

An Innovative Plan for Building Rockets

In building his rockets, Musk set out to use techniques for speed and cost control that he had learned in Silicon Valley. The plan was to manufacture the engines at the El Segundo site, but the rocket's body would be assembled from parts obtained elsewhere. Advances in computing and materials science would help his engineers fashion a rocket in record time. They loved the opportunity to tackle problems on a daily basis, without all the foot-dragging and bureaucratic holdups they had endured at the large aerospace firms. Musk kept his factory floor open, without segmenting the different types of work. Engineers and computer scientists mingled with machinists and welders. This allowed employees to share ideas and work out solutions more easily. When Musk discovered a freelance machinist who could make parts quickly and reliably to order, he hired him for his own team to cut out any delays.

Musk also urged his engineers to save time by building prototypes first, then testing them, tweaking them, and trying again. Each cycle—with its flaws and failures—moved them closer to the final product. This approach helped produce the crown jewel of the SpaceX rocket program: Tom Mueller's Merlin engine. Defying the skeptics, it was lightweight, remarkably efficient, and could generate 78,000 pounds of thrust—more than any privately developed rocket engine to date.

> **"Failure *was* an option at SpaceX, partly because the boss often asked the impossible of his team."[13]**
>
> —Eric Berger, science writer and expert on SpaceX's early history

Even though Musk was spending huge amounts of his own money on this venture, he encouraged his employees to take risks. "Failure *was* an option at SpaceX, partly because the boss often asked the impossible of his team," says Eric Berger, who has written about the company's early history. "In meetings, Musk might ask his engineers to do something that, on the face of it, seemed absurd. When they protested that it was impossible, Musk would respond with a question designed to open their minds to the problem, and potential solutions. He would ask, 'What would it take?'"[13]

The SpaceX workforce understood the massive challenge of building a workable rocket. Essentially, a rocket is a bomb filled with liquid fuels that combine to ignite the explosion of liftoff. Each part must be designed, manufactured, and assembled with great precision. The slightest error can bring about disaster. The internet is filled with videos of rockets exploding on the launch pad or veering off crazily after ignition.

But before the new company could conduct a test launch, Musk decided to promote his plans more publicly. Ever the showman, he hauled a prototype rocket across the country to Washington, DC, in December 2003. He parked it across the street from the National Air and Space Museum, like a heads-up about coming attractions. Sci-fi fans among the aerospace pros could appreciate the name of Musk's first rocket—Falcon 1, referring to Han Solo's *Millennium Falcon* in *Star Wars.*

Launch Failures and the Threat of Bankruptcy

On March 24, 2006, the first launch of the Falcon 1 rocket took place thousands of miles from SpaceX headquarters on a tiny island in the middle of the Pacific Ocean. Launches generally must be conducted near the ocean so that, in case of trouble, the rocket debris will fall safely into the water. The SpaceX team had logged an exhausting number of hours and jet miles preparing for the launch on Omelek Island in the Kwajalein Atoll. Every detail had to be covered. But inside the flight control room on another island, Musk kept asking one of his engineers about plans for the company's next rocket, so sure was he that the current launch would be a success.

Tension rose as the final seconds counted down. Musk and the crew watched as the blinding burst of ignition sent the Falcon 1 lifting into the air. Whoops of glee erupted in the control room. Then, just before the video feed cut off, the rocket began to roll to one side. Catching fire, it started to break apart, with flaming pieces spiraling into the water. The rocket booster was a total loss, although somehow its payload, a small satellite built by the US Air Force Academy, made it through undamaged. The whole episode shook the SpaceX crew. "It was amazing, and then it was horrifying," said operations manager Anne Chinnery. "Something like that, it hits you in the gut."[14]

Musk did not waste time worrying about the setback. He knew that other rockets had failed their early tests. By nightfall, he was joking with team members and making plans to move forward. However, the breakup of Falcon 1 proved to be the first of a string of failures. Falcon 1's second test in March 2007 reached space, but its second stage spun out of control until the engine burned out. On the third test in August 2008, a slight miscalculation in fueling caused the

> **"It was amazing, and then it was horrifying. Something like that, it hits you in the gut."[14]**
>
> —Anne Chinnery, operations manager for SpaceX

Starlink Pro and Con

Elon Musk's Starlink satellite network is designed to deliver low-cost internet to remote areas. As of November 2022, the network consisted of more than thirty-two hundred satellites. The idea is to offer connectivity to people who otherwise would have none. SpaceX officials say that Starlink will help isolated people access news, health services, and lifesaving information during natural disasters. Musk has also offered Starlink's service to the Ukrainian military in its fight against Russia's invading forces. Musk's supporters tout Starlink as a prime example of his humanitarian impulses, although the network also stands to generate billions in revenue.

Some scientists view Starlink as a nuisance and a possible danger. Astronomers worry that the array of bright objects in low orbit will interfere with their observations of the night sky. Scientists also fear that the sheer size and scale of the Starlink program will greatly increase the danger of collisions with other objects in Earth's orbit. "Starlink doesn't publicize all the maneuvers that they're making," says Hugh Lewis, Europe's leading expert on space debris. "But that causes problems for everybody else because no one knows where the satellite is going to be and what it is going to do in the next few days."

Quoted in Tereza Pultarova, "SpaceX Starlink Satellites Responsible for Over Half of Close Encounters in Orbit, Scientist Says," Space.com, August 20, 2021. www.space.com.

rocket's first stage to lurch forward and collide with its second stage just after separation.

All at once, the future of SpaceX looked bleak. The company was desperately in need of cash. Bankruptcy loomed as a very real outcome, and critics were speculating about Musk's imminent fall from grace. Everything depended on proving that SpaceX could put a commercial satellite into orbit. Working feverishly with little sleep, the team managed to set up a fourth test in a matter of weeks. The launch, on September 29, 2008, was a white-knuckle occasion like nothing that Musk and his team had ever experienced. This time the burn, launch, and separation all went off without a hitch. Nine and a half minutes after liftoff, the second-stage Kestrel engine shut down, sending the satellite payload safely into orbit. For the flight controllers, relief turned quickly to jubilation. Elon Musk had ridden his employees hard to reach this moment, and they had succeeded. From Kwajalein to El Segundo, for past employees and current staff, the party lasted deep into the night.

Launching the Falcon 9 and a NASA Bonanza

Suddenly, there was a cascade of good news for Musk and SpaceX. While the rest of the company was celebrating the Falcon 1 launch, a separate crew was working on the much larger Falcon 9 rocket, with its nine powerful Merlin engines stacked together in the booster. In November 2008 the crew test-fired the Falcon 9's engines for 178 seconds, long enough to simulate sending its first stage into space. Less than two years later, Falcon 9 would have its own successful launch.

As for the cargo it would carry, that was nailed down by a canny piece of lobbying and salesmanship in Washington, DC. The salesperson for SpaceX was Gwynne Shotwell, the company's

One of SpaceX's Falcon 9 rockets blasts off from its launch pad at Cape Canaveral on June 4, 2010.

vice president for business development. On her first interview with Musk six years before, he had been unimpressed and had hired her with some reluctance. Nonetheless, Shotwell went on to develop connections with government space agencies and the aerospace industry that would prove decisive. Although she was worried about making payroll back in Los Angeles, in meetings with top brass at NASA she made a convincing case for the Falcon 9 and her firm's capabilities. In December 2008 SpaceX was one of two companies awarded a contract with NASA to ferry supplies to the International Space Station. SpaceX's share was worth $1.6 billion.

The eye-popping deal arrived just in time. Musk did not hesitate to reward Shotwell's hard work and results that had defied the odds. He did not merely give her a raise; he made her the company's president. "He's funny and fundamentally, without him saying anything, he drives you to do your best work," says Shotwell. "He doesn't have to say a word. You just want to do great work."[15]

A Feat of Engineering Wizardry

Over the next several years, the Falcon 9 proved to be a reliable means for delivering payloads into space. But Musk was not satisfied with the status quo. He longed to achieve one of his earliest goals, which was to recover a booster, or first rocket stage, and reuse it a couple of months later for another launch. Such a step, which many aerospace veterans considered far-fetched at the time, would slash the cost of launching rockets by half, from more than $60 million to $30 million.

For Falcon 1 launches, SpaceX engineers had first experimented with parachutes to land the booster safely; upon reentering the atmosphere, however, the booster had always burned up before the parachutes could open. In 2012 the team developed and tested a better idea: a booster with a separate propulsion system for reentry. A single Merlin engine would throttle up as the booster hurtled back to Earth, slowing its descent and allowing for a soft landing.

It took months of trial and error, including a failed landing that came in too fast and exploded. But on December 21, 2015, the SpaceX team was able to bring in a Falcon 9 booster for a vertical landing on a concrete pad at Cape Canaveral. Several months later, the team did it again, this time landing the used rocket on the platform of a remote-controlled drone ship. Typical for Musk, he gave each drone platform its own whimsical name taken from starships in one of his favorite sci-fi novels, Iain M. Banks's *The Player of Games.* Landings were simply more fun when they touched down on mobile platforms named *Just Read the Instructions* or *Of Course I Still Love You*.

But those first landings were just a warm-up for an even more spectacular feat of engineering. On April 11, 2019, the Falcon Heavy, billed by SpaceX as the world's most powerful rocket, was ready for its first mission. At liftoff, its twenty-seven Merlin engines

On April 11, 2019, the two side boosters from a Falcon Heavy rocket glided down and executed an almost simultaneous landing on the launch pads with graceful precision. Within minutes, the third booster also nailed its landing on a drone platform 600 miles out to sea.

and 5 million pounds of thrust created a bone-jarring roar as it ascended into the sky. A few minutes later, after its payload had been released into orbit, the Falcon Heavy's two side boosters appeared overhead in the Florida twilight, with their reentry engines ignited. To the cheers of spectators watching the webcast at SpaceX mission control, the twin boosters glided down and executed an almost simultaneous landing on the launch pads with graceful precision. Within minutes, the third booster also nailed its landing on a drone platform 600 miles (966 km) out to sea. *Wired*'s technology reporter, Daniel Oberhaus, knew he had witnessed something amazing:

> Musk has long said that he will consider SpaceX successful when landing rockets becomes boring. But after watching the world's most powerful operational rocket go to orbit and then return each of its three first-stage boosters to Earth, I can't help but think that SpaceX will never be successful—at least not by Musk's metrics. The nearly simultaneous landing of the two side boosters is the most futuristic thing I have ever seen. In fact, one of the only things I can imagine that is more extraordinary than this feat of engineering would be treating it as mundane.[16]

A Vision That Continues to Grow

SpaceX rocket launches and landings may not have become boring, but they are certainly routine. As of early 2023, the Falcon 9 had completed 132 missions, generating billions in revenue from both government and private contracts. The windfall has enabled Musk to expand his vision for the company.

For example, SpaceX has made good on a plan dating back to January 2015 to place more than three thousand satellites in low Earth orbit. The project, called Starlink, is designed to provide secure internet connection from outer space. Currently,

> **"Is he going to inspire the next Elon Musk? That's the question. And if he can do that, then we win."[17]**
>
> —Jim Bridenstine, NASA administrator

Musk and his team are planning to deploy thousands more Starlink satellites in a network that could dominate internet service worldwide. A venture even closer to Musk's heart is Starship, an enormous reusable rocket that may one day carry up to one hundred humans and their necessary cargo to Mars. Tests of its prototype, Starhopper, ended successfully in 2019. Today, the company is in the midst of tweaking and testing new versions of Starship and its enormous Raptor engine. Plump rather than sleek, and fitted with a nose cone, landing fins, and a silvery stainless steel skin, Starship resembles the space vehicles in the classic books of science fiction that Musk loves. SpaceX already has a contract with NASA to develop Starship into a lander that can transport astronauts to the moon by 2030.

Elon Musk likes to joke that he wants to die on Mars—just not on impact. But experts on space travel believe that one of Musk's great achievements will be to inspire the next generation. NASA administrator Jim Bridenstine notes how the 1986 movie *Top Gun* spurred him to become a navy pilot, and he thinks Musk's SpaceX will have a similar effect. "That happened in my life and it changed my life," says Bridenstine. "Is he going to inspire the next Elon Musk? That's the question. And if he can do that, then we win."[17]

CHAPTER THREE

A Revolution in Electric Vehicles

Elon Musk's most celebrated business venture was not his own creation. The EV company Tesla Motors was originally the brainchild of engineers Martin Eberhard and Marc Tarpenning. The pair had made a nice profit on an early ebook company just before the dot-com bubble burst. Afterward, while shopping for a really fast sports car, Eberhard test-drove an EV1, a small, sporty EV made by General Motors. He was impressed by the vehicle's quiet ride and amazing acceleration—zero to sixty in nine seconds. Within a year, Eberhard and Tarpenning had pieced together a plan to build and sell their own high-dollar electric sports cars. On July 1, 2002, Tesla Motors was born. The name referred to Nikola Tesla, a Serbian American who had invented the electric motor.

What Eberhard and Tarpenning needed for their new enterprise was a deep-pockets investor with imagination. Musk was a leading candidate, as someone who had achieved his own dot-com success and who definitely loved the pursuit of innovation. They had been impressed by a speech Musk had made a couple of years earlier at a Mars Society event at Stanford. And, in fact, Musk was already looking to invest in an EV start-up. After a weekend meeting and a barrage of questions about Tesla's finances, Musk announced he was in.

Serbian American inventor and engineer Nikola Tesla works in his laboratory in New York. Tesla is credited with inventing the electric motor.

A Promising Debut

Investing in Tesla Motors enabled Musk to bring together several of his passions. He had long been hooked on sports cars of all kinds. Making an EV appealed to his environmental concerns about fossil fuels and global warming. Plus, he loved the notion of disrupting the automobile industry just as he was trying to shake up the commercial rocket industry with SpaceX. With an initial investment of $6.35 million in 2004, Musk found himself in the automobile business.

It was a notoriously difficult industry to crack. The last start-up to survive in the United States car business was Chrysler, which was founded in 1925. Industry experts, Wall Street analysts, and other carmakers laughed at Tesla's chaotic beginnings. But Musk saw potential in selling cutting-edge electric sports cars to rich people with an environmental conscience. And the luxury car market in the United States alone represented $3 billion a year in sales. He also believed that America and the world could eventually be swayed to buy EVs for everyday use. The rest would depend on hard work, engineering expertise, and a bit of luck. "What makes founders [such as Musk] so interesting is they have an idea that everyone tells them can't be done," says Lou Shipley, a professor of strategic management at Harvard and the Massachusetts Institute of Technology. "That's why he's having so much fun, because everybody thought he was wrong, and he's proving to be pretty right."[18]

One aspect of Tesla that especially appealed to Musk was its breakthrough in battery technology. With the help of engineer J.B. Straubel, the company was making use of the startling improvements in lithium-ion batteries, the kind used in laptop computers. The small batteries could be strung together in a battery pack to provide a much more potent charge. Tesla's first prototype, a sports car called the Roadster, ran on a 900 pound (408 kg) battery pack made up of 6,831 lithium-ion batteries. It could travel about 250 miles (402 km) on a single charge. It took three hours to recharge the batteries.

In July 2006 Tesla hosted a swanky event in a Santa Monica, California, airport hangar to unveil its new electric sports car. By then, Tesla Motors had become the darling of automotive and green technology enthusiasts. At the event, celebrities from Hollywood, business, and the political world could test-drive either of two Roadster prototypes, one red and one black. The two-seater convertibles, featuring sleek carbon-fiber bodies, could accelerate quietly from zero to sixty in about four seconds. With Musk holding court in an all-black tuxedo, guests were zipping back from their test-drives on the runway and opening up their checkbooks. For $100,000 up front, the company would reserve

> "What makes founders [such as Musk] so interesting is they have an idea that everyone tells them can't be done. That's why he's having so much fun, because everybody thought he was wrong, and he's proving to be pretty right."[18]
>
> —Lou Shipley, professor of strategic management at Harvard and the Massachusetts Institute of Technology

> "In keeping with a fast growing technology company, all free cash flow is plowed back into R&D [research and development]. . . . When someone buys the Tesla Roadster sports car, they are actually helping pay for development of the low cost family car."[19]
>
> —Elon Musk

a Roadster hot off the assembly line. Over the next few weeks, Tesla received several million dollars from wealthy Californians eager to get on the waiting list.

Shortly after the Santa Monica event, Musk posted his grand vision for Tesla on the company website. He explained that selling the Roadster was merely the first step to a much larger goal, that being an affordable EV. "In keeping with a fast growing technology company, all free cash flow is plowed back into R&D [research and development] to drive down the costs and bring the follow on products to market as fast as possible," he wrote. "When someone buys the Tesla Roadster sports car, they are actually helping pay for development of the low cost family car."[19]

From Investor to CEO

While basking in all the glowing media attention, Musk could see trouble ahead for Tesla. For one thing, its engineers and technicians had lost sight of the mission to keep costs down. Spreadsheets for production expenses and parts often included estimates, not real numbers, and the estimates tended to be too optimistic. The actual cost for producing a Roadster had ballooned to nearly $200,000.

Meanwhile, relations between Musk and Eberhard grew tense. Eberhard loved to spend the day on the factory floor working on technical matters with the other engineers. But Musk kept urging him to look at the larger financial picture. The key to Tesla's success, Musk told him, would be to prove it could manufacture EVs in large numbers and sell them for a profit. And that called for cheaper supplier networks, drastic cost-cutting measures, and a fanatical attention to details of performance and comfort.

Tesla EVs on Fire—Literally

In October 2013, just as Tesla was breaking out as a legitimate automaker, a new problem arose: battery fires. In one incident in Seattle, a Model S struck a metallic piece of debris on the road, puncturing the car's battery pack. Due to a warning about overheating from the car's computer, the driver was able to escape the vehicle unharmed. But in minutes the front of the car was engulfed in flames. When firefighters cut into the battery pack's safety firewall to spray it with water, they created holes that enabled the fire to spread from cell to cell. This caused the battery pack to erupt into a fiery inferno. Television newscasts around the country ran the footage from a passing motorist, making sure to mention that the EV was a Tesla.

When two more fires raised alarms, Tesla's stock price began to plummet. Musk hurried to explain in a blog post that the company had designed new undercarriage shields to protect the battery packs from road debris. He also stressed that gasoline cars catch fire too—and, on average, far more often than EVs. "Our three noninjurious fires got more national headlines than a quarter-million deadly gasoline-car fires," he told CNN. "That's mad! What the heck is going on?"

Quoted in Hamish McKenzie, *Insane Mode: How Elon Musk's Tesla Sparked an Electric Revolution to End the Age of Oil*. New York: Dutton, 2018, p. 42.

For example, Musk blasted the practical aspects of the Roadster, including details of performance, reliability, and comfort. The brief test-drives at the Santa Monica event had overheated the battery packs and nearly destroyed the cars. Battery packs that at first were air cooled had to be reworked to be liquid cooled. The suspension and braking systems also had to be redesigned. Musk even criticized the interior of the Roadster, noting that its features were far inferior to European luxury sports cars and its seats uncomfortable to boot. Tesla's engineers found Musk impossible to work with. They hated his constant sniping and claimed in private that his own changes would only add to the cost of the vehicle. Nonetheless, he was the boss, and nearly all of the changes were made.

Through it all, Musk tried to transfer the Roadster's improvements to the design of the Model S, the more moderately priced electric sedan that he saw at the time as Tesla's salvation. He worried that the company would run out of money before the

Model S could even reach production. It became obvious, not only to Musk but also to other Tesla investors, that Eberhard was not up to the job of CEO. In 2007 he was ousted from the helm just as Musk had been ousted at PayPal. The official reason was that Eberhard had misled Tesla's board of directors about cost overruns and production problems. He would hang on for a while before leaving the company entirely, as would Tarpenning. Eberhard remained bitter for years, and he later sued Musk for falsely claiming that he, not Eberhard and Tarpenning, had created the company. In 2009 Musk and Eberhard agreed to settle the suit by sharing cofounder credit with Tarpenning and two others. In public statements since then, Eberhard has merely indicated that Musk is a unique individual and a challenge to work with.

Years later, Musk would defend himself by pointing to the sacrifices he made for Tesla's success. "[Eberhard] plays the 'poor inventor' card, but was rich all along & invented nothing (as far as I know)," he posted on Twitter in 2020. "I went down to zero cash or sellable assets in 2008/2009, had no house & had to borrow money from friends to pay rent."[20]

Chaos at Work and at Home

Elon Musk was not exaggerating about the dire circumstances he faced after Eberhard's ouster. The Great Recession of 2008–2009, blamed on a meltdown in the US mortgage market, left struggling businesses such as Tesla scrambling to stay afloat. With SpaceX also strapped for cash, the economic crisis had Musk wondering which of his companies he should try to save, since saving both seemed impossible. He announced large layoffs at Tesla and stepped in as CEO. The company had already run through millions of dollars in deposits for the still unbuilt Roadsters, raising thorny questions of misuse of funds. Remaining Tesla employees woke up each morning hoping they still had a job. SolarCity, a solar panel maker that Musk owned, also was

Struggling to Make Self-Driving Cars

Elon Musk's quest to make nearly all of Tesla's vehicles capable of self-driving has hit multiple snags. He has hawked the company's Full Self-Driving Capability (FSD) for years, at one point predicting 1 million so-called robotaxis by the end of 2020. The reality, however, has fallen far short of his grand vision. Whereas he once promised a fully autonomous FSD, the system being tested today still requires a driver to be attentive and ready to take control if necessary. The goal of driverless vehicles remains years away.

The idea behind FSD is that Tesla's software Autopilot system makes safer driving decisions than a human operator. Musk believes that Autopilot's onboard cameras are sufficient for self-driving. But critics of the system, some of them former Tesla engineers, insist that more sensors are needed to make Autopilot safe enough for widespread use. They point out that the National Highway Traffic Safety Administration is investigating twelve accidents in which Teslas on Autopilot drove into police cars and emergency vehicles, resulting in one death and several injuries. "Where I get concerned is the language that's used to describe the capabilities of the vehicle," says Jennifer Homendy, chairwoman of the National Transportation Safety Board. "It can be very dangerous."

Quoted in Cade Metz and Neal E. Boudette, "Inside Tesla as Elon Musk Pushed an Unflinching Vision for Self-Driving Cars," *New York Times*, December 7, 2021. www.nytimes.com.

in desperate financial straits. Musk began selling his personal property to raise cash, including his house and sports cars. Silicon Valley bloggers seemed to revel in his misfortune. Followers of the tech industry flocked to a site called Tesla Death Watch for the latest bad news.

At the same time Musk's marriage was falling apart. Having created a large family in a short time (twins, and then triplets), the couple could not weather the onslaught of business pressures and private disagreements. Justine began her own blog in which she detailed her husband's patronizing treatment, impulsiveness, and workaholic ways. On the day Musk was supposed to arrange for marriage counseling, he filed for a divorce instead. Not long afterward, he began dating a young British actress named Talulah Riley. Fourteen years younger than Musk, she would soon become his second wife.

Second Wind from a Government Rescue

As so often happened in Musk's business career, financial help emerged just in time to avert a disaster. Musk knew that in order to survive, Tesla needed to roll out its less expensive Model S sedan and prove to investors and the public it was a genuine player in the automobile industry. In December 2008, he touted the Model S in interviews but added, "We can't move forward with that without a major amount of capital."[21] That is where the recent election of Barack Obama as president came in. The new administration was the godsend Musk needed. Obama's push for government funding for green businesses gave upstart Tesla a ray of hope.

In June 2010 Tesla Motors received a $465 million loan as part of the Obama administration's effort to aid development of clean-energy vehicles. Musk and Tesla officials used the money to purchase an empty Toyota factory in Fremont, California, as a manufacturing site. They also made plans for their own battery factory—Tesla's first so-called Gigafactory—in Sparks, Nevada. The new factory, a joint effort with the Japanese company Panasonic, would eventually open in 2016 and was essential in slashing the rising costs of lithium-ion batteries for Tesla's EVs. Other Gigafactories were planned for Buffalo, New York, and western Europe. The US Department of Energy (DOE) loan came on the heels of an agreement with German automaker Daimler to buy a 10 percent share of Tesla to develop smart EVs. Suddenly, Tesla was flush with cash and eyeing expansion. It also was able repay the DOE loan in only three years.

On June 29, 2010, Tesla Motors went public, enabling ordinary investors to buy shares in the company. One thing that investors liked about Tesla was its potential to make money from the federal government's environmental policies. For example, Tesla stood to profit from new federal fuel economy and carbon emissions standards. Makers of gas-powered cars that could not meet the new standards had to buy credits from companies that did, such as Tesla. Sales of these regulatory credits began to bring in more revenue every year. "In the early years of Tesla, this meant a lot," says David Rapson, an economics professor at the University of California, Davis. "These credits to the tune of billions of dollars would have been very beneficial in terms of relaxing their capital needs."[22] And the windfall has continued. In 2020 alone, Tesla banked $1.58 billion from selling emissions credits.

Musk and Tesla also benefited from government policies in other ways. In 2009 Congress created a $7,500 tax credit for EV buyers, thus reducing what wealthy buyers paid for a Tesla. In California, EV buyers could get an additional $2,500 state tax credit. And as Tesla expanded its building projects in the United States, city and state governments competed to see who could offer the company the largest tax breaks and incentives. The result was billions more in capital funding for Tesla.

A Breakthrough in Quality and Sales

Musk's crusade to normalize EVs received one of its first big boosts in 2013. That year *MotorTrend* magazine, one of the industry's most respected publications, named Tesla's Model S its Car of the Year. The Model S became the first EV to win the prestigious award. Even more important for American car

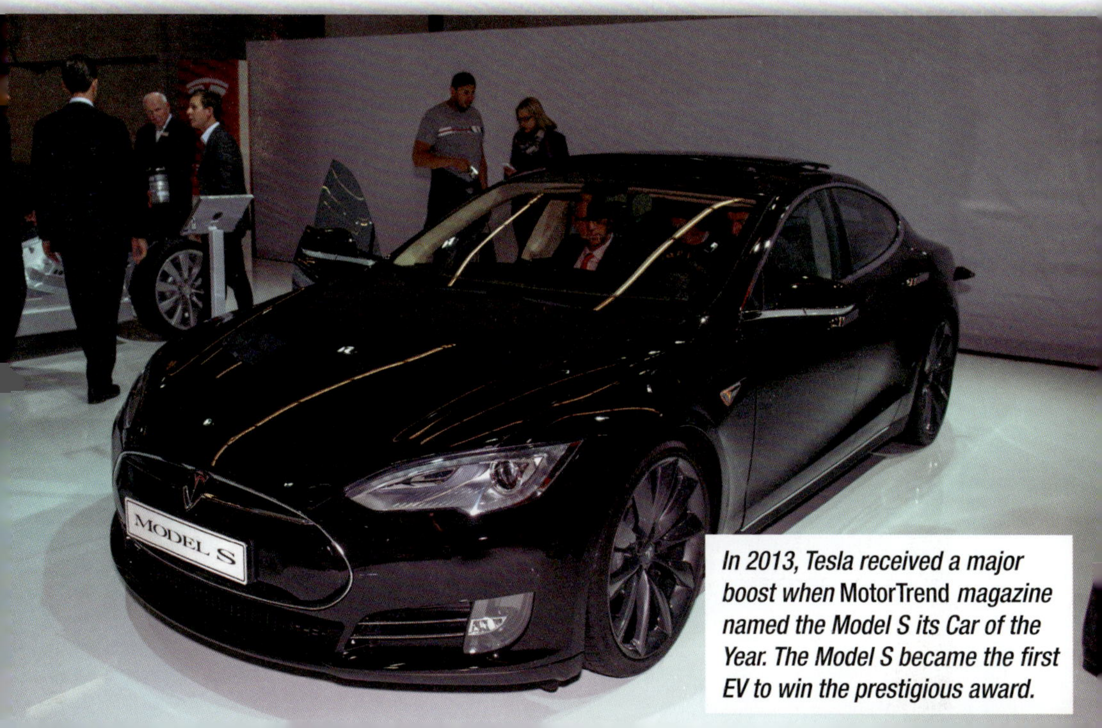

In 2013, Tesla received a major boost when MotorTrend *magazine named the Model S its Car of the Year. The Model S became the first EV to win the prestigious award.*

buyers was the glowing review that *Consumer Reports* gave the Model S. Its researchers were not automotive fans but hardheaded sleuths searching for the tiniest flaws in the vehicle. High grades from *Consumer Reports* served to convince buyers it was a practical car to purchase—at least if one could afford its $57,000 price tag.

Building on the momentum, Musk and the Tesla team met his ambitious goal to sell twenty thousand Model S cars in one year. Assembly-line problems held down sales the next year, but then the numbers resumed their climb. Stock analysts who had urged caution about Tesla and its flamboyant CEO began to change their tune. The stock price soared, vaulting Musk into the billionaire ranks. Announcement of a sales push into Europe and especially China hinted at more good news ahead. Tesla also unveiled plans for a Model X electric sport-utility vehicle and a lower-priced Model 3 family sedan. Supported by new Gigafactories, each the size of seventy-six football fields laid end to end, Tesla was closing in on Musk's dream of challenging the major carmakers. As Musk would tweet in 2021, "Luck is the best superpower."[23] But

Workers at a Gigafactory in China put the finishing touches on new Teslas in 2021. Each Gigafactory was the size of seventy-six football fields laid end to end.

it was also relentless hard work—his own and that of thousands of employees—that was paying off.

A Trillion-Dollar Company

For all the praise heaped on the Model S, it was the $35,000 Model 3 that shot Tesla's sales figures to undreamt-of heights. In July 2017 the company fielded orders for more than a half million of its new EV. By 2021, the Model 3 was the eighth-best-selling car in the world and the top-selling EV. That year Tesla sold a total of 936,000 cars. On October 25, 2021, Tesla's market value reached $1 trillion—more than the market values of Ford, General Motors, Honda, and Toyota *combined*. Musk himself edged past Amazon's Jeff Bezos to become the world's richest person.

> "Luck is the best superpower."[23]
>
> —Elon Musk

Musk's upstart EV company could no longer be dismissed by the legacy automakers. In fact, they pivoted to hawking their own EVs as the wave of the future. "There's no doubt, the auto industry is becoming much more serious about developing electric vehicles driven by the need for emissions compliance in the U.S., China and Europe," said Michael Robinet, an analyst for business information service IHS Markit. "Tesla has shown the industry that markets do exist for electric vehicles, and the major players have taken notice."[24]

Economic headwinds and political skirmishes have somewhat dimmed Tesla's outlook for now. But Elon Musk continues to pursue a seamless vision for Tesla, consisting of clean energy, emissions-free vehicles, and worldwide networks of Supercharger charging stations. A few years back, when it acquired the solar panel maker SolarCity, Tesla had dropped the word *Motors* from its name. The point was to emphasize that Tesla is more than just a car company. Where it goes next is largely up to Musk and his restless ideas for change.

CHAPTER FOUR

The Boring Company and Twitter 2.0

Sometimes Elon Musk can seem like a conglomerate all by himself. He owns two major companies, SpaceX and Tesla. He owns SolarCity (now called Tesla Energy). He also owns The Boring Company, Neuralink, and, most recently and controversially, the social media company Twitter. According to Business Insider, he has financial interests in at least seven more firms.

His businesses reflect the variety of his interests. Rather than focusing solely on making money, he claims to seek opportunities to both improve people's daily lives and benefit humanity in the long run. From local complications such as traffic gridlock to climate change and global problems, he does not shy away from a challenge. And unlike almost all of today's billionaires, Musk owes his wealth not to one big idea but to several ideas pursued successfully over the years. He rejects detailed business plans. Instead, he prefers to get the new enterprise up and running as quickly as possible and then react to any problems as they arise. And despite his impulsive nature, he has shown a remarkable ability to stay the course when a company seems on the verge of collapse. "When you first start a company, there's lots of optimism and things are great," he says. "Happiness, at first, is high. Then, you encounter all sorts of issues and happiness will steadily decline and you'll go through a whole world of hurt."[25]

Tunneling Under Traffic Jams

One of Musk's more outlandish business ideas came about from his frustration at being stuck in traffic in Los Angeles. While inching along in his Tesla one day in December 2016, he began to fantasize about a system of underground tunnels that could relieve the gridlock and get motorists moving again. He unloaded his irritation in a tweet: "Traffic is driving me nuts. Am going to build a tunnel boring machine and just start digging . . ."[26] For most people, that would have been the end of it, but Musk decided he had hit on something. In a series of tweets, he announced that he was actually going to start a tunneling business. He called it, with tongue firmly in cheek, The Boring Company (TBC). By February 2017 he was overseeing the first test dig in a SpaceX parking lot in Hawthorne, California. Over a long weekend, digging all day and all night, his workers produced an impressive hole that was 50 feet (15 m) wide and 15 (5 m) feet deep.

Musk tied his new tunneling idea to Hyperloop, which he had brainstormed several years before. Hyperloop was conceived as a tunnel-based system that would feature ultra-high-speed pods to move goods and people within and between large cities. The emphasis was on low-cost transportation that could avoid the worsening traffic gridlock. TBC would create separate tunnels for cargo and automobile traffic at a fraction of the cost of building new roads.

Musk has developed the idea by dividing the company's services into five categories: Loop, Utility, Freight, Pedestrian, and Bare. Loop, also known as "Teslas in Tunnels," is a high-speed all-electric underground public transport system that zips passengers to their destinations without stops. Utility employs the tunneling system to handle utility lines, allowing for easy repairs without disrupting traffic on the surface. Freight creates tunnels for

> "When you first start a company, there's lots of optimism and things are great. Happiness, at first, is high. Then, you encounter all sorts of issues and happiness will steadily decline and you'll go through a whole world of hurt."[25]
>
> —Elon Musk

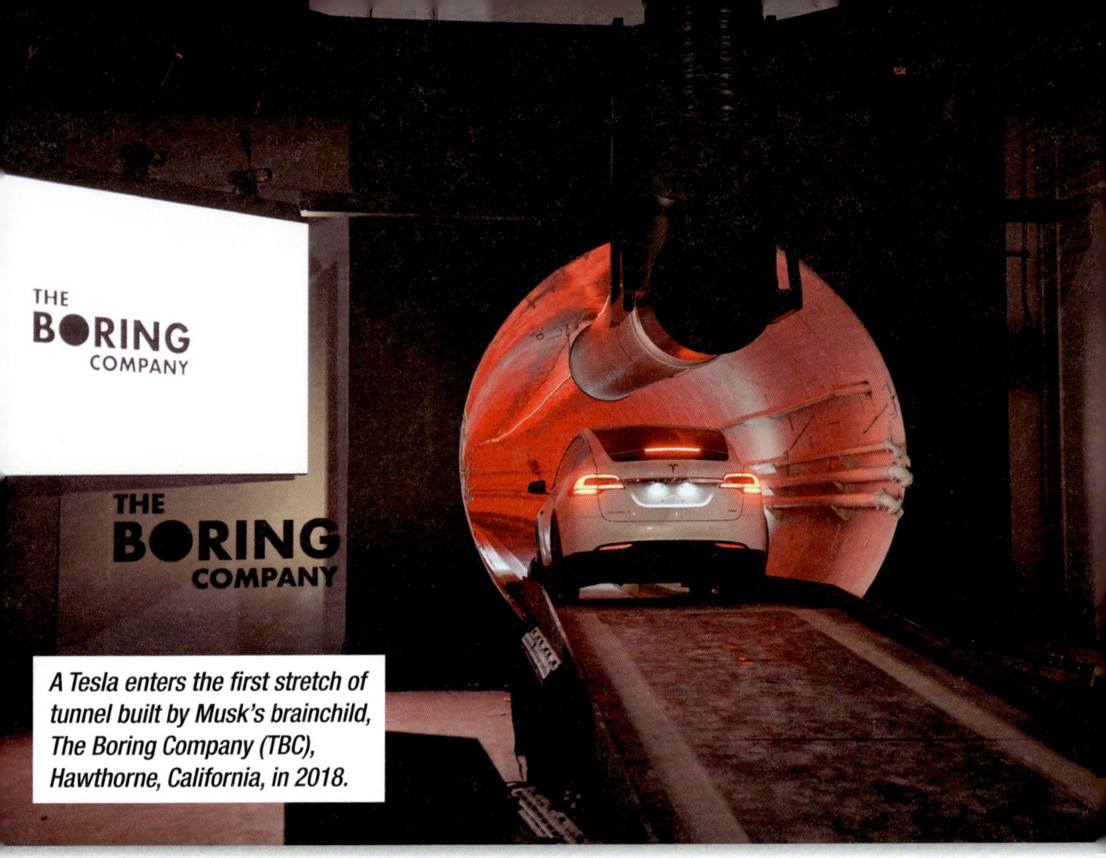

A Tesla enters the first stretch of tunnel built by Musk's brainchild, The Boring Company (TBC), Hawthorne, California, in 2018.

hauling cargo. Pedestrian offers tunnels for safe foot travel. And Bare, the most curious offering, enables a purchaser to repurpose a bare tunnel in whatever way is desired.

TBC finished its first stretch of underground tunneling in Hawthorne on December 18, 2018. However, as has often happened, Musk had promised more than he could deliver. There were no high-tech passenger pods racing through the tunnel at 150 miles per hour (241 kph). Instead, the vehicles were standard Teslas traveling along tracking wheels like cars through a car wash, at speeds no faster than 50 miles per hour (80 kph). Passengers on the test run complained of a bumpy ride.

Falling Short of the Hype

At first, Musk had no problem getting contracts for his new enterprise. In June 2018 TBC won a bid competition to build a high-speed loop system from downtown Chicago to O'Hare Airport. Musk's plan called for automated EVs, each carrying sixteen passengers with luggage, to leave every thirty seconds at speeds of more than 100 miles per hour (161 kph). In May 2019 TBC signed a $48.7 million deal to create an underground "people mover" tunnel for the Las Vegas Convention Center and its 200 acre (81 ha) layout. TBC also made ambitious tunnel plans for Ontario International Airport in California; for a Hyperloop connection between Baltimore and Washington, DC; and for tunnel systems in Los Angeles and San Bernardino, California. Successful completion of the Chicago project alone stood to earn TBC as much as $16 billion.

However, Musk and TBC have mostly fallen far short of the initial hype. The Las Vegas project is one of the few that have been completed. Elsewhere, city and state officials have bought into Musk's rule-breaking reputation and grandiose plans only to end up with nothing to show for it. In Ontario, Musk had promised that TBC could build a 4-mile-long (6 km) underground tunnel for only $45 million, compared to the estimated $1 billion for a street-level rail system. But, in the end, TBC failed to even submit a bid by the January 2022 deadline. The company's proposal to create a Hyperloop in Chicago hit snag after snag, then fell through altogether when Mayor Rahm Emanuel, the project's main booster, left office. Time and again, Musk and TBC have failed to negotiate the maze of permits and regulations needed to go forward. Sometimes they have simply lost interest. Chicago alderman Scott Waguespack was skeptical about TBC and the Hyperloop project from the start. "It was a lot of flash and dash," says Waguespack, "and not any kind of public discussion about whether it was even necessary or not."[27]

A Bid for Twitter

Throughout his career as a tech entrepreneur and public figure, Elon Musk has carried on a conversation with his fans and detractors via the social media platform Twitter. With more than 100 million followers, he ranks with former president Obama as one of the most-followed figures on the site. He has used his Twitter account to rail at government regulations, make bold predictions about his companies, jab back at his critics, toss off silly jokes, and comment on current events.

Musk had often told his followers on Twitter that he might one day create his own rival social network. In 2022, however, he set his sights on Twitter itself. Musk has called himself a free-speech absolutist, meaning he believes in as few restrictions on speech as possible. He considers free speech to be the basis for a healthy democracy. His own frequent run-ins with Twitter's rule makers and in-house censors had convinced him that the platform was far from the open forum for different viewpoints that it claimed to be, especially for conservatives. Not only did Musk disagree with Twitter's speech policies, but he also believed the site was failing badly as a moneymaking enterprise. With his usual bravado, he was certain that he could make improvements in both areas.

In late January he began to buy large blocks of shares in the company. By April, he had acquired a 9 percent stake, worth nearly $3 billion, making him Twitter's largest individual shareholder. Musk made it clear that he was out to change the way Twitter operated. He joined the company's board and signaled his intention to influence its decisions. Twitter CEO Parag Agrawal was careful not to criticize the move. "He's both a passionate believer and intense critic of the service which is exactly what we need on @Twitter, and in the boardroom, to make us stronger in the long-term," Agrawal said in a tweet. "Welcome Elon!"[28]

A Messy Acquisition

The good feelings did not last long. When Musk announced his intention to buy Twitter outright, the board scrambled to block the deal. It employed a so-called poison pill strategy, allowing shareholders to buy cheap new Twitter shares. This diluted Musk's stake in the company and made his buyout more expensive. Nevertheless, he would not be deterred. In mid-April he agreed to

Linking Computers and the Human Brain

The Musk company that has received the least media attention is Neuralink. Musk cofounded it in 2016 with the objective of developing links between the human brain and computers. The idea is to implant a device in a person's skull that can enhance that person's natural abilities or treat disorders. For example, in extreme cases, a brain-computer interface might enable a paralyzed person to walk again.

Although all this may sound like the science fiction Musk loves, he stresses its practical benefits. "The reality is that almost everyone over time will develop brain and spine problems," says Musk. "These range from minor to very severe, but if you live long enough, basically everyone's going to have some neurological disorder." And he adds, "Neurons are like wiring. And you kinda need an electronic thing to solve an electronic problem."

After years of initial trials on monkeys, Neuralink announced human clinical trials for its brain chip technology beginning in 2023. The trials will focus on restoring vision, even in patients blind since birth, and helping paralysis victims regain muscle movement.

Quoted in Manas Sen Gupta, "Tesla and All Other Companies Led by Elon Musk and What They Do," *Lifestyle Asia*, December 14, 2022. www.lifestyleasia.com.

purchase Twitter for $44 billion—a price some analysts said was far too high.

In July, Musk tried to back out of the deal. He claimed that Twitter had misled him about the number of fake automated accounts, or bots, on the platform. Subtracting these meant that the site actually had far fewer regular users than advertised. Stock experts suspected he might be trying to negotiate a lower purchase price. But in a sagging market for tech stocks, Twitter's board and shareholders were now anxious to complete the sale. Twitter sued Musk to hold him to his original agreement. In October, facing a possible billion-dollar penalty should the ruling go against him, he closed the deal.

Upon taking ownership, Musk immediately displayed his eccentric sense of humor. He hauled a sink into Twitter headquarters in San Francisco and tweeted "entering Twitter HQ—let that sink in!"[29] He updated his profile on Twitter to read "Chief Twit."[30] He also tweeted a concise comment on the future: "the bird is freed."[31] Later, in an open letter to Twitter's advertisers, he tried to strike a reassuring note: "The reason I acquired Twitter is because it is important to the future of civilization to have a common digital town square, where a wide range of beliefs can be debated in a healthy manner, without resorting to violence. . . . That said, Twitter obviously cannot become a free-for-all hellscape, where anything can be said with no consequences."[32]

Layoffs and a Chaotic Transition

Musk's takeover of Twitter generated plenty of angst among its employees and many liberal users across the country. He hit the ground running, taking Agrawal's place as CEO and also firing the head of content policy, Vijaya Gadde. Within days he had laid off about half of Twitter's seventy-five hundred employees worldwide, many of whom said they had not received customary offers of severance pay. Many more Twitter employees resigned in protest. Fired employees complained via Twitter that they had been locked out of their company email accounts. One software engineer who survived the first wave of layoffs was let go after he tweeted questions about Musk's leadership. Some observers wondered whether the company's dwindling staff would even be able to keep the platform running. Musk warned employees who remained that long hours of work at high intensity would now be the norm. As he was used to doing at SpaceX and Tesla, Musk himself regularly worked until two or three in the morning to see that his demands were being met. Twitter 2.0, as he called the transition, would require everyone's total commitment.

> "The reason I acquired Twitter is because it is important to the future of civilization to have a common digital town square, where a wide range of beliefs can be debated in a healthy manner. . . . That said, Twitter obviously cannot become a free-for-all hellscape, where anything can be said with no consequences."[32]
>
> —Elon Musk

Musk seemed determined to outrage his critics. As he had promised, he reinstated former president Donald Trump's account,

Following his purchase of the social media platform Twitter, Musk reinstated the account of former president Donald Trump, who had been previously banned for violating Twitter's code of conduct.

although Trump declined to use it. Trump, some other conservatives, and some progressives had been banned from the site for violating Twitter's code of conduct. These additional banned users also regained access. According to outside content monitors, the site saw a jump in trolling, misinformation, and hate speech of various kinds. Media Matters, a left-leaning media watchdog, reported a 500 percent increase in racist language. A proposed new blue-check system to verify top-rated accounts was put on hold, leading to a wave of impostors and satirical accounts. Throughout, Musk kept blasting the former administrators of Twitter as partisan hacks and its workers as coddled slackers. *The Atlantic*'s Tom Nichols noted, "For the past few days, Elon Musk has been throwing a gigantic temper tantrum on his platform, Twitter. It is not usually a matter of public interest when a narcissist like Musk goes haywire, but just as Donald Trump's anger warped our public

> "For the past few days, Elon Musk has been throwing a gigantic temper tantrum on his platform, Twitter. It is not usually a matter of public interest when a narcissist like Musk goes haywire, but . . . Musk's conniptions could affect our culture and how we get information."[33]
>
> —Tom Nichols, writer for *The Atlantic*

life, Musk's conniptions could affect our culture and how we get information."[33]

Such sentiments spread to corporate America. Brands such as General Mills and Volkswagen, fearful of having ads appear next to questionable content, decided to pause their advertising on Twitter. Hollywood stars, including Whoopi Goldberg and Jim Carrey, led the exit of disgusted users to other message sites. Musk admitted that revenues were falling fast, blaming the drop on political activists. He took an emergency all-hands-on-deck approach, calling on software engineers from SpaceX and Tesla to help make changes to the platform. Amid the chaos, critics predicted Twitter's demise. "It's unlikely to fail all at once," said Robert Reich, the former US secretary of labor, "but bugs and glitches will mount, the quality of what's offered will deteriorate, hateful tweets will burgeon, and customers and advertisers will flee."[34]

A Social Media App That Does Everything

Elon Musk's ultimate vision for Twitter goes far beyond its current status as a messaging platform. In some ways, his ideas look back to the beginning of his tech career and X.com, a proposed online banking app that was cut short by the PayPal buyout. He wants to include a payment system on Twitter and enable users to connect their digital bank accounts to the platform. He also hopes to move the company into debit cards, checking, currency exchanges, stock trading, and other financial services.

Eventually, Musk says, Twitter could become a so-called everything app, modeled on the Chinese platform WeChat. Users could access features for getting news, hailing rides, ordering food and merchandise, and making and viewing videos. Above all, Musk wants to be open to new possibilities. "The rate of evolution of Twitter will be an immense step change compared to what it has been in the past," Musk says. "You know, if nothing else, I am a technologist and I can make technology go fast. And that's what you'll see happen at Twitter."

Quoted in Tiffany Hsu and Kate Conger, "On Twitter, Elon Musk Details His Plans for Twitter's Business," *New York Times*, November 9, 2022. www.nytimes.com.

Opening the Twitter Files

But the forecasts of doom for Musk's Twitter 2.0 proved premature. By the end of November, the site's user numbers were growing, especially in the United States. Analysts noted that downloads of the Twitter app had increased 23 percent since Musk's takeover and 42 percent from the previous year. Musk could boast that he was bringing new life to the platform.

His next move promised to attract even more attention. In December, Musk announced that he was opening Twitter's email archives to some handpicked independent journalists so they could investigate the platform's decisions to ban certain users and prevent tweets on certain subjects from being shared. Musk believed that the treatment of conservatives on the platform had amounted to censorship, perhaps even illegal muzzling of free speech. Musk hyped the release of the so-called Twitter Files by claiming, "Twitter is both a social media company and a crime scene."[35]

The Twitter Files, presented as a series of tweets on different subjects, unveiled the inner workings of Twitter's content control. One series showed how company officials acted to suppress a *New York Post* story about the overseas business dealings of Hunter Biden, the son of then-presidential candidate Joe Biden. Another series dealt with allegations of shadow banning, in which the tweets of certain users, mostly political conservatives and critics of the federal government, were prevented from being shared on the platform. For example, Jay Battacharya, a well-respected epidemiologist at Stanford University, was shadow banned for his posts challenging the wisdom of COVID-19 policies, including lockdowns and school closings.

A Talent for Disruption

Regardless of how his acquisition of Twitter turns out, Musk has shown once more his supreme talent for disruption. In mid-December 2022 he conducted a Twitter poll about whether he

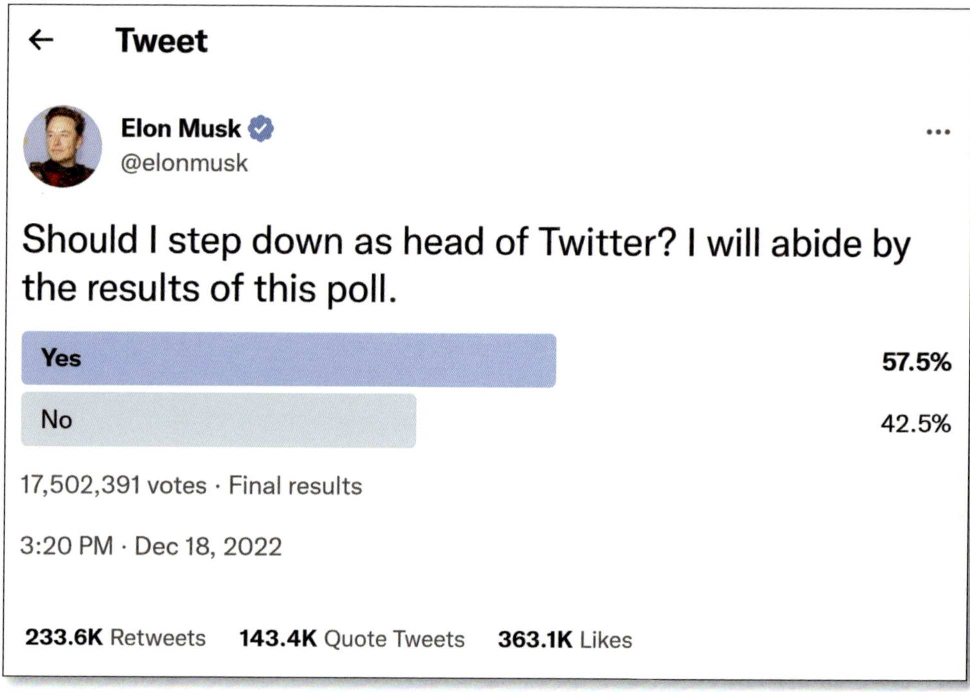

In 2022, Musk conducted a Twitter poll in which he asked whether he should step down as the social media company's CEO, promising to abide by the results. Fifty-seven percent of Twitter users said that Musk should step down.

should step down as the company's CEO. He pledged to abide by the results. Fifty-seven percent voted for Musk to fire himself, which may have come to him as a relief. As CBS News reported, "Musk said he never intended to be CEO of Tesla, and he didn't want to be chief executive of any other companies either, preferring to see himself as an engineer instead."[36]

SOURCE NOTES

Introduction: A Tech Wizard Out to Save the World

1. Quoted in Jason Douglas and Alexa Corse, "Elon Musk Talks of 'Too Much Work on My Plate,' After Twitter Takeover," *Wall Street Journal,* November 14, 2022. www.wsj.com.
2. Quoted in Adam Mann, "SpaceX Now Dominates Rocket Flight, Bringing Big Benefits—and Risks—to NASA," *Science,* May 20, 2020. www.science.org.
3. Quoted in Suzy Weiss, "Elon Musk's Die-Hard Fans Believe the Wacky Billionaire Can Do No Wrong," *New York Post,* July 8, 2020. www.nypost.com.
4. Quoted in Alan Ohnsman, "Rupert Murdoch 2.0: How Twitter Gives Elon Musk the Power to Shape Public Opinion," *Forbes,* November 3, 2022. www.forbes.com.

Chapter One: From South Africa to Silicon Valley

5. Quoted in Neil Strauss, "Elon Musk: The Architect of Tomorrow," *Rolling Stone,* November 15, 2017. www.rollingstone.com.
6. Quoted in Jason Duaine Hahn, "Inside the Complicated Relationship Between Elon Musk and His Estranged Father, Errol Musk," *People,* March 26, 2018. www.people.com.
7. Quoted in Ashlee Vance, *Elon Musk: Tesla, SpaceX, and the Quest for a Fantastic Future.* New York: HarperCollins, 2015, p. 41.
8. Quoted in Vance, *Elon Musk*, p. 49.
9. Quoted in Zaini Majeed, "Elon Musk Responds to His University of Pennsylvania Homework; Here's What He Said," Republic world.com, June 14, 2021. www.republicworld.com.
10. Quoted in Ryan Mac, Cade Metz, and Kate Conger, "'I Don't Really Have a Business Plan': How Elon Musk Wings It," *New York Times,* October 28, 2022. www.nytimes.com.
11. Quoted in Taylor Locke, "Why Elon Musk Says Taking 'Vacations Will Kill You,'" *CNBC,* November 2, 2019. www.cnbc.com.

Chapter Two: The Pursuit of Commercial Space Travel

12. Quoted in Vance, *Elon Musk*, p. 101.
13. Eric Berger, *Liftoff: Elon Musk and the Desperate Early Days That Launched SpaceX.* New York: HarperCollins, 2021, p. 25.
14. Quoted in Berger, *Liftoff*, p. 88.
15. Quoted in Catherine Clifford, "President of SpaceX: This Is What It's Like Working for Elon Musk," CNBC, May 16, 2018. www.cnbc.com.
16. Daniel Oberhaus, "SpaceX Lands All 3 Boosters of the World's Most Powerful Rocket," *Wired,* April 11, 2019. www.wired.com.
17. Quoted in *CBS News,* "Elon Musk Praises NASA Astronauts for Their 'Nerves of Steel' Ahead of Historic SpaceX Launch," May 27, 2020. wwwcbsnews.com.

Chapter Three: A Revolution in Electric Vehicles

18. Quoted in Dominick Reuter, "A Harvard and MIT Professor Explains How Tesla Went from a Laughing Stock on Wall Street to Become the Most Valuable Car Company in the World," Business Insider, July 20, 2020. www.businessinsider.com.
19. Elon Musk, "The Secret Tesla Motors Master Plan (Just Between You and Me)," Tesla blog, August 2, 2006. www.tesla.com.
20. Quoted in Katharine Schwab, "Did Elon Musk Steal Tesla? Here's Why the CEO Is Rebutting Long-Time Allegations on Twitter," *Fast Company,* October 12, 2020. www.fastcompany.com.
21. Quoted in Brian Eckhouse, "Tesla Wouldn't Be Tesla Without Stimulus Spending," Bloomberg, June 8, 2020. www.bloomberg.com.
22. Quoted in Maggie Stevens, "Elon Musk Hates Government Subsidies. His Companies Love Them," Grid, April 30, 2022. www.grid.news.
23. Quoted in Hannah Grace, "Elon Musk Reveals the 'Best Superpower'—and It's Not the Power of Flight to Go to Space," iTechPost, October 19, 2021. www.itechpost.com.
24. Quoted in Meghan Reeder, "Tesla CEO Elon Musk's Influence Grows as Automakers Roll Out Electric-Vehicle Plans in Detroit," CNBC, January 16, 2019. www.cnbc.com.

Chapter Four: The Boring Company and Twitter 2.0

25. Quoted in Marcel Schwantes, "Elon Musk Says Adopting These 3 Simple Steps Has Helped Produce His Success," *Inc.,* January 24, 2020. www.inc.com.

26. Quoted in Adario Strange, "Elon Musk Seems Serious About Creating a Boring Company to Solve Traffic," Mashable, December 17, 2016. www.mashable.com.
27. Quoted in Ted Mann and Julie Bykowicz, "Elon Musk's Boring Company Ghosts Cities Across America," *Wall Street Journal,* November 28, 2022. www.wsj.com.
28. Quoted in Max Zahn, "A Timeline of Elon Musk's Tumultuous Twitter Acquisition," ABC News, November 11, 2022. www.abcnews.go.com.
29. Quoted in Beatrice Nolan, "Elon Musk Tweets 'the Bird Is Freed' Amid Reports He Plans to Take Twitter CEO Role," Business Insider, October 28, 2022. www.businessinsider.com.
30. Quoted in Fatma Khaled, "Why Did Elon Musk Buy Twitter? New Letter Reveals Reason," *Newsweek,* October 27, 2022. www.newsweek.com.
31. Quoted in Nolan, "Elon Musk Tweets 'the Bird Is Freed' Amid Reports He Plans to Take Twitter CEO Role."
32. Quoted in Joshua Robertson, "Elon Musk Says He's Going to 'Help Humanity' by Buying Twitter," The Gamer, October 27, 2022. www.thegamer.com.
33. Tom Nichols, "The Childish Drama of Elon Musk," *The Atlantic,* December 16, 2022. www.theatlantic.com.
34. Robert Reich, "Elon Musk Went on a Firing Frenzy at Twitter. Now He's Paying for It," *The Guardian,* November 21, 2022. www.theguardian.com.
35. Vanya Gautam, "Elon Musk Hints at Revealing Twitter's Darkest Secrets After Calling the Company a 'Crime Scene,'" *India Times,* December 12, 2022. www.indiatimes.com.
36. CBS News, "Twitter Users Vote Overwhelmingly in Poll for Musk to Step Down as CEO," December 19, 2022. www.cbsnews.com.

IMPORTANT EVENTS IN THE LIFE OF ELON MUSK

1971
On June 28, Elon Reeve Musk is born in Pretoria, South Africa.

1989
Musk immigrates to Canada and attends Queen's University in Kingston, Ontario.

1992
Musk moves to the United States to attend the University of Pennsylvania, where he earns degrees in economics and physics.

1995
After moving to Silicon Valley in California, Musk and his brother, Kimbal, start Zip2, a web software company that provides online city guides.

1999
In February, Compaq buys Zip2 for $307 million, earning Musk $22 million.

2000
In October, Musk is fired as chief executive officer (CEO) of PayPal, a position he had held since April 2000.

2002
In May, Musk founds SpaceX, a rocket and space exploration company.

2004
In February, Musk adds to his investment in the electric vehicle company Tesla and joins its board of directors.

2006
Musk's wife, Justine, gives birth to triplet sons—Kai, Saxon, and Damian.

2007

After Tesla's founder, Martin Eberhard, is ousted, Musk becomes the company's CEO.

2008

After three failed launches, SpaceX's Falcon 1 rocket successfully delivers a satellite payload into orbit.

2012

In May, SpaceX's Dragon vehicle docks with the International Space Station for the first time. SpaceX is the first commercial company to accomplish this.

2014

Tesla announces construction of the Gigafactory in Nevada, where it will make its own lithium-ion batteries.

2015

For the first time, SpaceX brings in a Falcon 9 booster for a vertical landing at Cape Canaveral, Florida.

2018

Musk tweets that he plans to take Tesla private, setting off a stock-buying frenzy and drawing fines and sanctions from the US Securities and Exchange Commission.

2019

SpaceX launches its first sixty Starlink satellites, creating a network for secure internet connection from outer space.

2020

Musk and his girlfriend, the singer Grimes, have a son together, whom they name X AE A-Xii—X for short.

2021

Sales of Tesla's Model 3 continue to rise, Tesla stock soars, and, for a time, Musk becomes the world's richest person.

2022

After months of negotiations and attempts to back out, Musk completes a deal to buy the social media platform Twitter for $44 billion.

FOR FURTHER RESEARCH

Books

Eric Berger, *Liftoff: Elon Musk and the Desperate Early Days That Launched SpaceX*. New York: HarperCollins, 2021.

Tim Higgins, *Power Play: Tesla, Elon Musk, and the Bet of the Century.* New York: Doubleday, 2021.

Hamish McKenzie, *Insane Mode: How Elon Musk's Tesla Sparked an Electric Revolution to End the Age of Oil.* New York: Dutton, 2018.

Jimmy Soni, *The Founders: The Story of PayPal and the Entrepreneurs Who Shaped Silicon Valley.* New York: Simon & Schuster, 2022.

Ashlee Vance, *Elon Musk: Tesla, SpaceX, and the Quest for a Fantastic Future*. New York: HarperCollins, 2017.

Internet Sources

Kenneth Chang, "SpaceX Lifts NASA Astronauts to Orbit, Launching New Era of Spaceflight," *New York Times,* November 10, 2021. www.nytimes.com.

Manas Sen Gupta, "Tesla and All Other Companies Led by Elon Musk and What They Do," Lifestyle Asia, December 14, 2022. www.lifestyleasia.com.

Daniel Howley, "How Elon Musk Changed Tesla," Yahoo! Money, April 8, 2022, http://money.yahoo.com.

Ryan Mac, Cade Metz, and Kate Conger, "'I Don't Really Have a Business Plan': How Elon Musk Wings It," *New York Times,* October 28, 2022. www.nytimes.com.

Adam Mann, "SpaceX Now Dominates Rocket Flight, Bringing Big Benefits—and Risks—to NASA," *Science*, May 20, 2020. www.science.org.

Dominick Reuter, "A Harvard and MIT Professor Explains How Tesla Went from a Laughing Stock on Wall Street to Become the Most Valuable Car Company in the World," *Business Insider*, July 20, 2020. www.businessinsider.com.

Websites

Brookings Institution

www.brookings.edu

The Brookings Institution is a nonprofit public policy organization based in Washington, DC. It conducts in-depth research to help solve problems facing society at the local, national, and global level. Its website features many articles and analyses about Elon Musk and his companies' impact on the United States and the world.

Hoover Institution

www.hoover.org

The Hoover Institution is a public policy think tank that seeks to improve the human condition by advancing ideas that promote economic opportunity and prosperity. Its website features many articles and discussions about policy and technology issues, including some about Elon Musk.

NASA Spaceflight

www.nasaspaceflight.com

This NASA website provides a wide variety of information about spaceflight, including articles about SpaceX and its various initiatives.

SpaceX.com

www.spacex.com

The company website describes its core mission as launching vehicles capable of carrying humans to Mars and other parts of the solar system. The site features videos of the company's recent rocket launches and landings and includes updates about other SpaceX projects.

TechCrunch

http://techcrunch.com

This technology website describes its mission as helping founders and start-up teams get ahead. The site focuses on the latest news from technology start-up companies, as well as technology breakthroughs in general. It includes regular updates and critical discussions on Musk's companies and the technologies they are pursuing.

Tesla

www.tesla.com

The company website provides information about Tesla products and the latest news stories about the company. The site also describes ways that its customers can advocate for clean energy and innovations such as Tesla's Supercharger car-charging network.

INDEX

PICTURE CREDITS

Cover: Brian Lawless/ZUMAPRESS/Newscom

6: J Marshall-Tribaleye Images/Alamy Stock Photo
9: ARCHIVIO GBB /Alamy Stock Photo
10: Radu Bercan/Shutterstock
17: Associated Press
20: NASA
26: UPI/Alamy Stock Photo
28: PR images/Alamy Stock Photo
32: IanDagnall Computing/Alamy Stock Photo
39: lexan/Shutterstock
40: Xinhua/Alamy Stock Photo
44: Reuters/Alamy Stock Photo
49: Tero Vesalainen/Shutterstock
52: Apex MediaWire/Alamy Stock Photo

ABOUT THE AUTHOR

John Allen is a writer who lives in Oklahoma City.